The Wilson's Family Adventure!

Written by Drayton & Lauryn Walker Illustrated by Izzy Bean

Copyright © 2017 by Drayton & Lauryn Walker
All rights reserved. This book or any portion thereof
may not be reproduced or used in any manner whatsoever
without the express written permission of the publisher
except for the use of brief quotations in a book review.

Limits of Liability and Disclaimer of Warranty
The author and publisher shall not be liable for your misuse of this material. This book is strictly for informational and educational purposes. The purpose of this book is to educate and entertain. The author and/or publisher do not guarantee that anyone following these techniques, suggestions, tips, ideas, or strategies will become successful. The author and/or publisher shall have neither liability nor responsibility to anyone with respect to any loss or damage caused, or alleged to be caused, directly or indirectly by the information contained in this book.

Illustrations by Izzy Bean (www.izzybean.co.uk)

Views expressed in this publication do not necessarily reflect the views of the publisher.

Printed in the United States of America

ISBN 978-1-948270-02-1

Keen Vision Publishing, LLC
www.keen-vision.com

From Parents to Parents

As military families, constant moving, sporadic changes, and distance from our loved ones is a way of life. While we know what is expected from the life we chose, it is sometimes difficult to separate from our families, especially when children are involved. Though we are proud to serve our country, our children don't always understand the uprooting and replanting. It can be especially difficult when they have to leave their friends and everything they love to start all over again. Major transitions can sometimes cause children to become numb and lose a desire to connect with their environments. In fact, studies show that because of their parents' commitment to the military, many military children are impacted socially and have a hard time making lasting connections even once they enter adulthood. For that reason, as parents who serve this great nation, we must do all that we can to ensure that our children not only have a voice, but are also as fairly involved in the process as possible. That's why Youlanda and I encouraged our children to start this series, *The Wilson's Family Adventure*.

We are excited to share our military family experience in a forum that highlights the kids' perspective. *The Wilson's Family Adventure* is a series catered to military children. This series is special to us because it communicates our children's thoughts about our professional choices. As a dual military family, Youlanda and I take great care in communicating with Drayton and Lauryn to ensure they have buy-in as it pertains to family decisions. The kids get to vote on duty stations and voice opinions about what they endure as we transition in the military from place to place. We develop calendars with timelines of events to establish predictability in their lives. Since military life has a propensity to add unhealthy stress to an otherwise normal life, we intentionally carve out family time. This time does not include the kids' activities or the parents' activities. This is time for the entire family to talk and have real fun. Everyone gets to be a kid (again!), any topic is open for discussion, and everyone is allowed uninterrupted time. Many people say, "Children are resilient." Well, we do not believe they should have to be resilient. We want them to be children and do child-like activities for as long as possible. We attempt to maintain a balanced lifestyle. God is the center of our family, so our balance stems from a continual relationship of prayer and church.

We pray our journey is a vehicle for military parents to communicate with their children. Within this series, our children communicate about the things we did as a family to prepare for transitions. If you've never included your children in the process before, don't be discouraged. Allow our adventure to open the door for conversations about how they feel now and even how they've felt in the past. It's never too late to implement new and improved systems that will help your children become healthy, successful, and whole. So, welcome aboard The Wilson's Family Adventure! We hope you enjoy it.

Yours truly,

Darrell and Youlanda Walker

From Kids to Kids

Hey there! We are so excited to share our adventures with other military children. Our book series, The Wilson's Family Adventure is just for military children like us whose parents serve this great country! Moving is really hard. We have to leave our friends, go to a new school, leave our house, and everything we are familiar with. We have to get on planes which can be really scary if it's your first time. If you ever feel sad about having to move, it's okay! All military kids like us feel that way sometimes. When we feel like this, we have to make sure that we talk about how we feel instead of keeping it all in.

When we have to move, we do a few things that make our move easier. We get phone numbers, email addresses, social media information, and other things to keep in touch with the friends we have to leave. This lets us stay in touch with our old friends when we make new friends. It helps us not miss them as much. We even have packing parties with our friends! There are so many cool things you can do to make moving time easier. We will share them with you in *The Wilson's Family Adventure* series!

Remember, you are not alone! There are a gazillion of military children across the world. It may be hard to leave everything you know and love, but a new place means a new adventure and more people to meet. A lot of children never get to travel or see the world, but as military kids, we get to experience more places than many people do in their entire lives. It may seem hard, but we are really blessed! If moving is going to be fun, we have to change the way we look at it! We hope that *The Wilson's Family Adventure* series helps you with that!

Well, that's all for now! We hope you like our books!

Love,

Drayton & Lauryn Walker

For Military Families Across the World!

Hello! I am Eli. This is my sister, Maria.
Here are our parents, Chris and Sunflower.

We are a military family. Our dad is in the Army. Our mom is in the Air Force. I am in the 3rd grade. Maria is in the 2nd grade.

For now, we live in Oklahoma.
Follow us as we learn about our next home.

One day at dinner, Dad made a very important announcement. "Guess what, gang?" Dad said. "We are moving!"

"Moving? When? Where? Nooo! I like our house. I don't want to leave my friends. What about gymnastics? I can't leave now. I just learned to flip!" Maria cried.

"I just earned my green belt in Tae Kwon Do!" I shouted. "Master Yun said I can have my black belt in a few years if I keep at it. I can't leave now!"

"Kids! Kids! Please settle down," Dad said. "Our new place will have all of that and more. Here, look at this brochure. Do you see the pictures? The Army and Air Force are moving us to Los Angeles, California."

"When do we go? How long will we be there? We don't want to move!" Maria and I said.

"Calm down, guys. We have 90 days left here. We will be in Los Angeles for three years, just as we've done here," Dad explained.

No matter what Dad said
or how fun the pictures looked,
we were not happy. We were very, very sad.
This would be our third time moving.

"The children are not happy about leaving Oklahoma," Mom said. "They love it here. I love it here. Is there anything we can do?"

Dad hugged Mom and said, "I would do anything for you guys." Maybe we can make the move a real family adventure! Let's do something to get the kids involved with the transition to Los Angeles!"

"That's a great idea," said Sunflower. "What do you think, kids?"

Maria and I looked at each other and smiled.

"You guys will love Los Angeles just as much as you love Oklahoma." Dad said.

"Yes," Mom agreed. "This adventure will fun!"

"Well, what do we do first?" I asked.

"First," Dad said, "We need to think about our new house.

"I want a big house with my own room, a yard, and a pool! I want a blue room!" I said.

"I want a pink room," Maria said. "Oh yeah, with a puppy. I want a pink room with a puppy!"

"Puppies do not come with the house," I said to Maria.

"Well, can I have a tree house?" Maria asked.

"Yeah, a tree house would be fun," I agreed. "I'm sure Dad can build it for us!"

As Maria and I discussed the details of the house, our parents just looked at us and laughed. Our family adventure was beginning to be so much fun for everyone.

Later that night, Dad showed us some cool pictures of Los Angeles. He showed us a huge Hollywood sign.
Dad said that a lot of famous people live in Los Angeles. He also said that Los Angeles also had a Disney Land.
Maria and I got very excited as we learned about all the fun things we could do in Los Angeles.

Next, we had to pick our two favorite toys to take on the plane ride. Last time we moved, we couldn't find Maria's favorite toy bird, Bluey. Maria cried for months until Mom found him. Now when we move, we make sure we take our two favorite toys on the plane with us so they do not get lost.

Maria and I began to think about all our friends. We were very sad about leaving them. Dad told us to make a contact sheet with all of our friends' information. When we got to Los Angeles, we could write or call them. Dad even said we could send them a card from our new home! This made us very happy. Maria and I had many friends at church, school, and our neighborhood. We had to use a lot of paper to write them all.

On Monday morning, we were the first to arrive at the bus stop! We could not wait to tell our friends that we were moving. When we told them the news, they were very sad.

We exchanged numbers and addresses with our friends. Our lists grew very fast. Some of our friends even gave us gifts to remember them. My friend, Zaria, gave me an friendship bracelet. Maria's friend, Abigail, gave Maria her favorite doll. Abigail and Maria had been friends since preschool. They were very sad to leave each other, but promised to keep in touch.

At church on Sunday, we told our church family about the big move. Everyone was very sad. Our Sunday School teacher decided that we would have a going away party. This made everyone very happy.

The days went by very fast. It was almost time to move. We had to pack, but Maria and I did not know what to take with us. "Maria and Eli, let's use this checklist to pack our things!" Mom said.

The checklist sorted our things into three piles: things to go in boxes for Los Angeles, things to go to charity, and things we would take on the airplane. The checklist made packing very easy. Mom is so smart. We finished packing and sorting our things.

We spent the rest of the night looking at new houses, schools, and cool places to visit in Los Angeles.

Finally, it was time to go! The movers came and packed our things. We loaded our car and headed to a hotel. We would stay at the hotel for four days until it was time to board our airplane.

"I don't like moving, but I love staying in hotels!" Maria said.

"Yeah, my favorite part is room service," I said. "Mom, can I call for room service when we check in?"

"But, you're not hungry, Eli." Mom said.

"I will be once we get all of these bags into the room!" I said. Mom laughed.

"Let's just wait until we get settled, Eli." Mom said. "Besides, we have a going away party to attend tonight. You don't want to ruin your appetite!"

Mom was right.
Our Sunday School teacher,
Ms. Berry, made the best snacks.
We would really miss her.

Our going away party was amazing! We received so many gifts. We also had a blast with our friends. I did my secret handshake with Justin, one of my best friends. Maria and her friends chatted all night about the amazing things we would see in Los Angeles. When we left the party, we were very sad. Mom and Dad reminded us about our adventure, and we were happy again. We would miss our friends so much, but there was so much fun in store for our family! On the way to the hotel, we talked about all the awesome things we would do in Los Angeles.

Finally, it was time to board the airplane. Mom and Dad said they had a special surprise for us. On the way to the airport, we stopped at a restaurant. Instead of going through the drive-thru, Mom and Dad let us go inside to eat and play. When we walked in, we saw our friends! They had all come to see us before we left! We took pictures and had a blast until it was time to leave.

It finally hit us that we were leaving our friends.
Maria and I began to cry.

"Don't look so sad," Daddy said. "We will be at the airport soon! You guys know how much fun we have at the airport!"
Maria and I loved to go to the airport. I wanted to be a pilot, so I loved to meet the pilots and the crew. As we made our way to our gate, Maria made silly jokes.
"Mommy, why did the chicken cross the road?"
"I don't know, Maria." Mommy laughed. "Why did the chicken cross the road?" "Because the cab was waiting on the other side!" Maria giggled. We all laughed. Maria was so silly. She made us laugh the entire time. We almost forgot we were leaving what had been our home for 3 years.
As we settled into our seats, we sighed.
It was finally time for us to leave.
"Hey gang!" Daddy smiled. "Are you ready for the Wilson Family adventure?"
"Yes!" Maria and I cheered.
As the plane took off, we looked out the window, we waved goodbye to Oklahoma.
"Goodbye, Oklahoma! We'll miss you!" Maria and I said.

About the Authors

Hey there! My name is Drayton. I am 10 years old, and I was born in Kansas City, Kansas. I'm really good at Taekwondo, dancing, and acting. I also enjoy reading, skating, and playing tag with my kid sister, Lauryn. One day, I'd like to be a famous actor and a Blue Angels Pilot. I have a bright future ahead of me and I'm excited about it!

Hi! My name is Lauryn, and one day, I'm going to be a famous singer and gymnastics coach! I was born in Bethesda, Maryland. Now, we live in Huntsville, AL. I LOVE reading, hanging out with my big brother, Drayton, and playing with my school and neighborhood friends.

STAY CONNECTED

Thank you for purchasing *The Wilson's Family Adventure!* Drayton and Lauryn would like to connect with you. Below are a few ways you can stay connected with them!

FACEBOOK www.facebook.com/TheWilsons.FamilyAdventure

EMAIL dlw2connect@gmail.com

WEBSITE www.dlw-connect.com

Made in the USA
Monee, IL
24 March 2021